Copyright 2023. All rights reserved. No part of this book or this book as a whole may be used, reproduced, or transmitted in any form or means without written permission from the publisher.

www.ingramcontent.com/pod-product-compliance
Lightning Source LLC
Chambersburg PA
CBHW062113220526
45471CB00010B/3722